Editor
Lorin Klistoff, M.A.

Managing Editor
Karen Goldfluss, M.S. Ed.

Editor-in-Chief
Sharon Coan, M.S. Ed.

Cover Artist
Barb Lorseyedi

Art Coordinator
Kevin Barnes

Art Director
CJae Froshay

Imaging
Rosa C. See

Product Manager
Phil Garcia

Publisher
Mary D. Smith, M.S. Ed.

Brain Teasers

GRADE 3

Author

Mary Rosenberg

Teacher Created Resources, Inc.
6421 Industry Way
Westminster, CA 92683
www.teachercreated.com

ISBN: 978-0-7439-3753-5

©*2003 Teacher Created Resources, Inc.*
Reprinted, 2009
Made in U.S.A.

Table of Contents

The old adage "practice makes perfect" can really hold true for your child and his or her education. The more practice and exposure your child has with concepts being taught in school, the more success he or she is likely to find. For many parents, knowing how to help your children can be frustrating because the resources may not be readily available. As a parent it is also difficult to know where to focus your efforts so that the extra practice your child receives at home supports what he or she is learning in school.

This book has been designed to help parents and teachers reinforce basic skills with children. *Practice Makes Perfect* reviews basic math skills for children in grade 3. This book contains 43 brain teasers that allow children to learn, review, and reinforce math concepts. Brain teasers have long proved their worth as vehicles of learning. Such activities carry with them curiosity and delight. While it would be impossible to include all concepts taught in grade 3 in this book, the following basic objectives are reinforced through the brain teasers:

- adding single and double digits
- subtracting double digits
- multiplying single digits
- using division
- finding the factors

- solving and creating equations
- recognizing number patterns
- using logic
- using operations
- finding odd and even numbers

How to Make the Most of This Book

Here are some useful ideas for optimizing the activity pages in this book:

- Set aside a specific place in your home to work on the activity pages. Keep it neat and tidy with materials on hand.

- Set up a certain time of day to work on the brain teasers. This will establish consistency. Look for times in your day or week that are less hectic and more conducive to practicing skills.

- Keep all practice sessions with your child positive and constructive.

- Help with instructions, if necessary. If your child is having difficulty understanding what to do or how to get started, work through the first problem with him or her.

- Review the work your child has done. This serves as reinforcement and provides further practice.

- Allow your child to use whatever writing instruments he or she prefers. For example, colored pencils can add variety and pleasure to the activity page.

- Pay attention to the areas in which your child has the most difficulty. Provide extra guidance and exercises in those areas.

- Look for ways to make real-life applications to the skills being reinforced.

Brain Teaser 1

Sharply Dressed Dog

This dog is getting ready for a party, but he needs help with color. Color the odd numbers red and the even numbers blue. Then color the rest of the dog brown.

Brain Teaser 2

Fifty-Fifty

Color the numbers greater than 50 orange and the numbers less than 50 green.

Circle the numbers larger than 50.

81	86	99	94
42	25	63	89
47	5	13	82

Circle the numbers smaller than 50.

54	10	57	33
98	14	19	29
73	75	77	44

Brain Teaser 3

Flowering Factors

Color the factors for 12 red and the remaining numbers green.

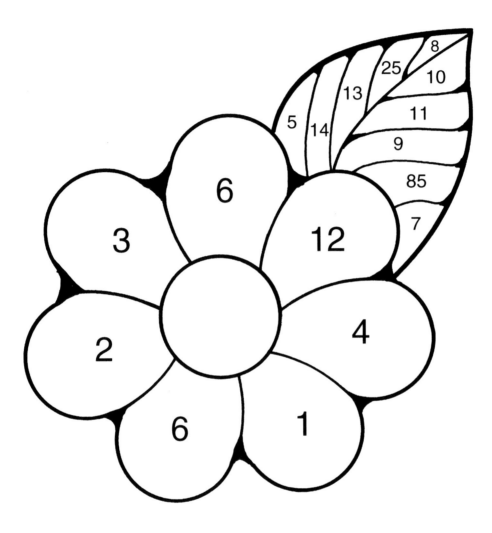

Circle the factors for 16.

3	4	9	7
5	6	8	2

Circle the factors for 20.

10	2	8	9
3	7	5	4

Brain Teaser 4

On the Road with Factors

Color the factors for 18 blue and the remaining numbers black.

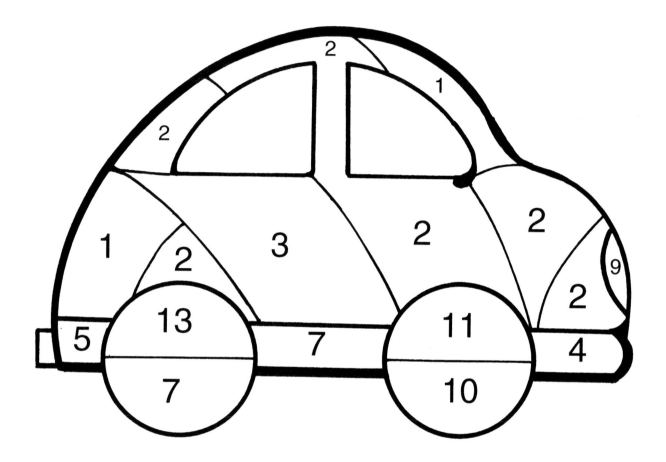

Write the factors for each number.

1. 4: _____

2. 6: _____

3. 9: _____

4. 10: _____

5. 15: _____

Brain Teaser 5

Number Trivia Set A

Solve each trivia problem.

1. Number of digits in a phone number x number of digits in an area code

_____

2. Number of digits on a clock + number of digits on a phone

_____

3. Number of digits on a ruler – number of digits on a dice

_____

4. Number of digits on a calculator ÷ number of digits in a zip code

_____

5. Current year x number of digits in a year (Example: 2002) _____

6. Birth year – birth date _____

7. Number of digits in an area code + number of digits in a phone number

_____

8. Add together all of the digits in your area code and phone number

_____

9. Current year – birth year _____

10. Current age x date of birth_____

Brain Teaser 6 ෮ ෯ ෮ ෯ ෮ ෯ ෮ ෯ ෮ ෮ ෯

Number Trivia Set B

Solve each problem.

1. Number of legs on a dog x number of tails on a dog

_____

2. Number of eyes on a cat x number of paws on a cat

_____

3. Number of octopus legs ÷ number of ears on a pig

_____

4. Number of legs on a bug x number of legs on a spider

_____

5. Number of body parts on an insect x number of body parts on a spider

_____

6. Number of legs on a bird ÷ number of beaks on a bird

_____

7. Number of legs on an octopus – number of feet on a hamster

_____

8. Number of horns on a bull x number of horns on a hen

_____

9. Number of legs on a slug + number of legs on a fish

_____

10. Number of wings on a bat + number of tongues on a snake

_____

Brain Teaser 7 ꙮ ꙮ ꙮ ꙮ ꙮ ꙮ ꙮ ꙮ ꙮ ꙮ ꙮ

Number Trivia Set C

Solve each trivia problem.

1. Number of nickels in a quarter + number of pennies in 6¢

_____

2. Number of dimes in $1 − number of quarters in $1

_____

3. Number of pennies in 25¢ ÷ number of nickels in 5¢

_____

4. Number of half-dollars in 50¢ x number of dimes in 50¢

_____

5. Number of quarters in 75¢ x number of quarters in $1

_____

6. Number of nickels in 30¢ − number of dimes in 30¢

_____

7. Number of pennies in 10¢ − number of pennies in one dime

_____

8. Number of quarters in 25¢ + number of nickels in 25¢

_____

9. Number of dimes in 90¢ ÷ number of nickels in 15¢

_____

10. Number of silver dollars in $1 x number of pennies in $1

_____

Brain Teaser 8

Number Trivia Set D

Solve each trivia problem.

1. Number of months in one year x number of days in one week

   _____

2. Number of months in one year ÷ number of days in a weekend

   _____

3. Number of holes in a donut x number of holes in a piece of binder paper

   _____

4. Number of peanuts in a shell x number of eggs in a dozen

   _____

5. Number of cookies in one dozen ÷ number of sodas in a 6-pack

   _____

6. A set of triplets x total number of fingers on two hands

   _____

7. Number of toes on both feet x number of fingers on both hands

   _____

8. Number of legs on a tripod – number of eyes on a Cyclops

   _____

9. Number of days in one year + number of months in a decade

   _____

10. Number of days in one week – number of days in a weekend

    _____

Brain Teaser 9

Block Out 12

Color the factors for 12. Each set of factors must be touching at least one side or corner. Each number can only be used one time.

Examples: <u>6</u> x <u>2</u> = 12 and <u>3</u> x <u>2</u> x <u>2</u> = 12

4	3	6	4	6	6	6	3
3	6	2	4	3	2	4	4
6	6	2	4	2	3	2	4
4	3	6	3	2	2	4	3
2	2	4	6	3	2	3	6
3	4	2	3	2	2	2	4
2	2	2	3	3	2	6	6
2	3	4	6	6	4	6	4

© *Teacher Created Resources, Inc.*

Brain Teaser 10

Block Out 18

Color the factors for 18. Each set of factors must be touching on at least one side or corner. Each number can only be used one time.

Examples: $\underline{3}$ x $\underline{3}$ x $\underline{2}$ = 18 or $\underline{6}$ x $\underline{3}$ = 18

9	3	2	3	3	6	3	9
2	2	6	9	6	2	2	3
2	6	3	9	2	3	9	2
3	6	3	6	2	3	2	9
6	2	3	2	3	9	6	3
6	9	2	6	2	3	6	2
9	2	3	9	3	3	2	9
3	2	2	9	3	6	2	3

Brain Teaser 11

Block Out 24

Color the factors for 24. Each set of factors must be touching at least one side or corner. Each number can only be used one time.

Examples: $\underline{2} \times \underline{3} \times \underline{4} = 24$

4	4	6	8	3	2	8	6
3	3	8	2	6	6	3	6
4	2	6	4	6	4	3	2
8	4	4	8	2	8	8	3
2	8	2	6	6	3	4	4
4	6	8	2	3	6	2	4
6	2	4	3	8	2	8	3
2	3	8	3	4	3	6	2

Brain Teaser 12

Block Out 30

Color the factors for 30. Each set of factors must be touching at least one side or corner. Each number can only be used one time.

Examples: $\underline{2}$ x $\underline{5}$ x $\underline{3}$ = 30

2	5	3	4	4	2	4	3
5	3	6	2	5	4	2	5
2	4	4	3	5	3	4	3
6	5	3	6	3	2	6	5
2	4	2	6	2	6	5	4
5	6	4	5	6	5	2	3
3	6	3	6	3	6	6	5
4	2	6	3	4	2	5	2

Brain Teaser 13

Jar of Jelly Beans

Read the clues to figure out how many of each color of jelly beans there are in the jar. Then answer the questions below.

Clues

- There are 20 red jelly beans in the jar.

- There are 10 fewer white jelly beans than yellow jelly beans.

- There are half as many orange jelly beans as red jelly beans.

- There are 5 more pink jelly beans than red jelly beans.

- There are 10 more black jelly beans than green jelly beans.

- There are twice as many yellow jelly beans as red jelly beans.

- There are 5 fewer green jelly beans as red jelly beans.

Orange jelly beans:_____   Yellow jelly beans:_____

Green jelly beans:_____   Pink jelly beans: _____

Black jelly beans: _____   White jelly beans: _____

1. Which two colors of jelly beans have the same amount in the jar?

_____ and _____

2. What is the total number of jelly beans in the jar? _____

3. Are there more red and yellow jelly beans or black and white jelly beans?

_____

Brain Teaser 14

Perfect Puzzles #1 and #2

Place each number in the crossword puzzle—one digit in each box. Each number can be used one time.

Example Puzzle

43	104
51	128
85	197

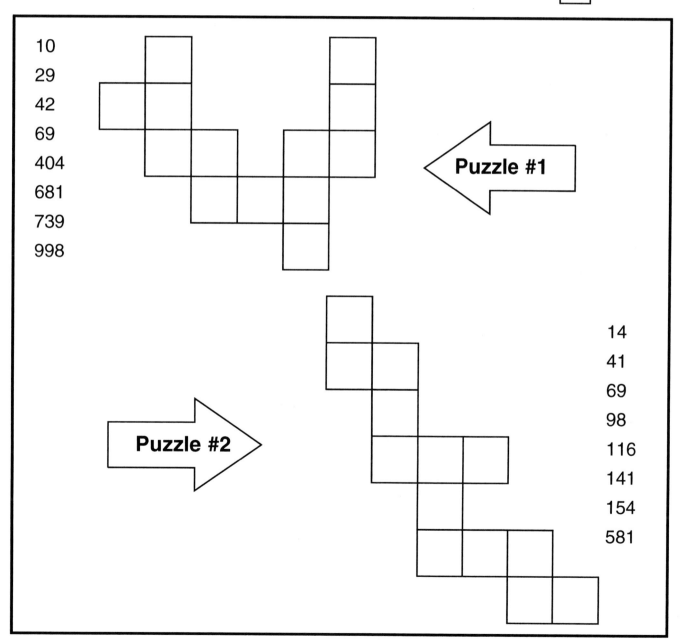

10
29
42
69
404
681
739
998

Puzzle #1

Puzzle #2

14
41
69
98
116
141
154
581

Brain Teaser 15

Perfect Puzzles #3 and #4

Place each number in the crossword puzzle—one digit in each box. Each number can only be used one time.

Example Puzzle

43	104
51	128
85	197

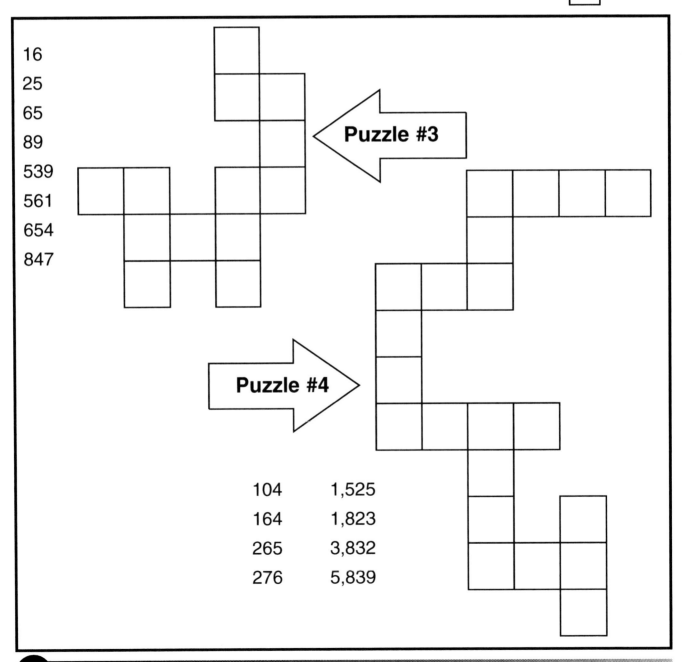

16	
25	
65	
89	
539	
561	
654	
847	

104	1,525
164	1,823
265	3,832
276	5,839

Brain Teaser 16

Perfect Puzzle #5

Place each number in the crossword puzzle—one digit in each box. Each number can be used one time.

Example Puzzle

43	104
51	128
85	197

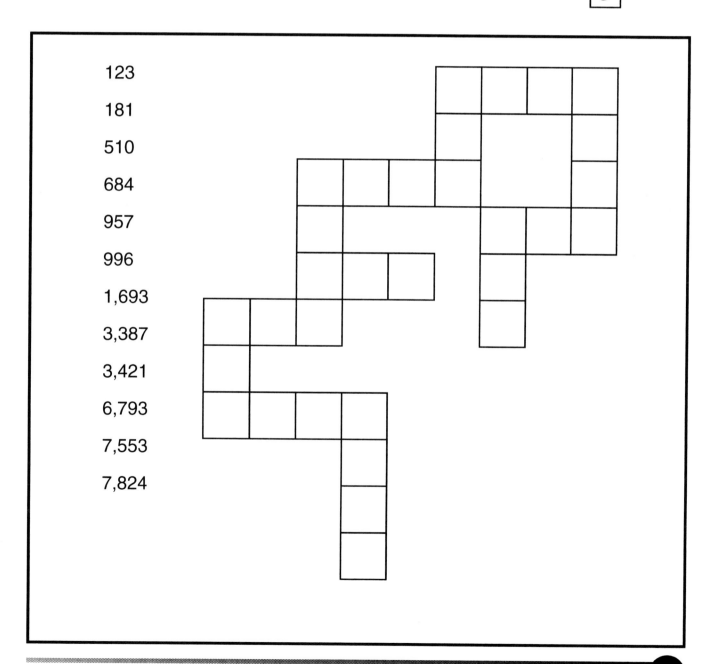

123

181

510

684

957

996

1,693

3,387

3,421

6,793

7,553

7,824

Brain Teaser 17

Perfect Puzzle #6

Place each number in the crossword puzzle—one digit in each box. Each number can be used one time.

Example Puzzle

43	104
51	128
85	197

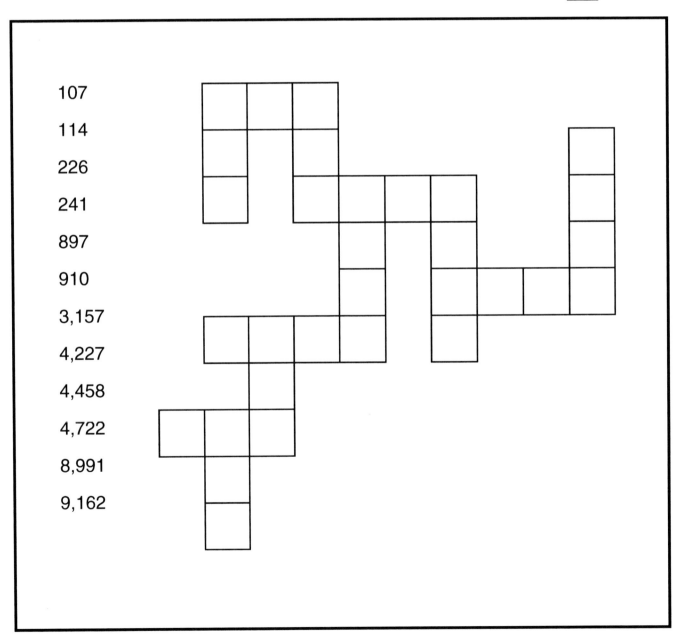

107

114

226

241

897

910

3,157

4,227

4,458

4,722

8,991

9,162

Brain Teaser 18

Perfect Puzzle #7

Place each number in the crossword puzzle—one digit in each box. Each number can only be used one time.

Example Puzzle

43	104
51	128
85	197

2,575   7,518   42,913

3,346   8,547   68,691

4,351   28,861   76,931

6,239   36,501   91,010

Brain Teaser 19

Piggy Banks

Read each clue. If the answer is "yes" make an "O" in the box. If the answer is "no" make an "X" in the box. Then fill in the correct answer below.

	$1.00	$5.00	$10.00	$20.00	$50.00
Angel					
Clyde					
Cybil					
Ty					
Val					

Clues

- Val has more than $1.00 but less than $20.00.
- Clyde has the most money.
- Angel has more money than Cybil.

- Cybil has more money than Val.
- Ty has the least amount of money.

 Clyde has _____.   Val has _____.   Angel has _____.

 Cybil has _____.   Ty has _____.

Brain Teaser 20

Roller Blades

Read each clue. If the answer is "yes" make an "O" in the box. If the answer is "no" make an "X" in the box. Then fill in the correct answer below.

	$1.19	$1.29	$1.39	$1.49	$1.59
Celia					
Charles					
Libby					
Lorne					
Bo					

Clues

- Libby spent more than $1.50 for her roller blades.
- Bo spent 30 cents less on his roller blades than Libby did.
- Celia spent less than Bo.
- Charles spent more than Lorne for his roller blades.

 Charles spent _____.

 Bo spent _____.

 Lorne spent _____.

 Libby spent _____.

 Celia spent _____.

Brain Teaser 21

Lucky Numbers

Read each clue. If the answer is "yes" make an "O" in the box. If the answer is "no" make an "X" in the box. Then fill in the correct answer below.

	18	29	37	41	47	88
Travis						
Mavis						
Emilio						
Sarah						
Selina						
Henry						

Clues

- Emilio's lucky number is not the largest or the smallest numbers.
- Selina's lucky number is an even number.
- Travis' lucky number is an odd number.
- Sarah's lucky number is larger than 40.
- Henry's lucky number is less than 40.
- Mavis' lucky number is divisible by 3.
- Travis' lucky number is larger than Sarah's.
- Emilio's lucky number is smaller than Henry's.

 Henry's lucky number

 Travis' lucky number

 Mavis' lucky number

 Selina's lucky number

 Emilio's lucky number

 Sarah's lucky number

Brain Teaser 22

Mystery Circles Set A

Each circle has a specific value—for example 2, 3, or 4. The sum is where two (or more) circles overlap. Find the value of each circle. Study the example below.

Example: Values—2, 3, 4

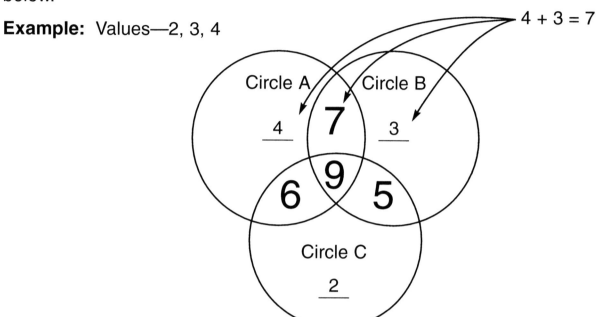

$4 + 3 = 7$

Values—1, 2, 3

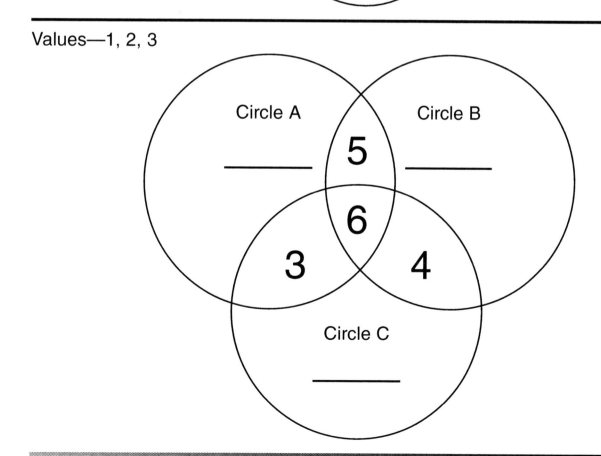

Brain Teaser 23 ⟳ ⟲ ⟲ ⟳ ⟲ ⟳ ⟲ ⟳ ⟲ ⟳ ⟳ ⟲

Mystery Circles Set B

Each circle has a specific value—for example 2, 3, or 4. The sum is where two (or more) circles overlap. Find the value of each circle. Study the example below.

Example: Values—2, 3, 4

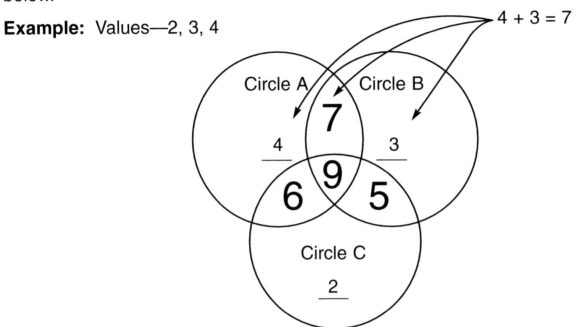

$4 + 3 = 7$

Values—5, 6, 7

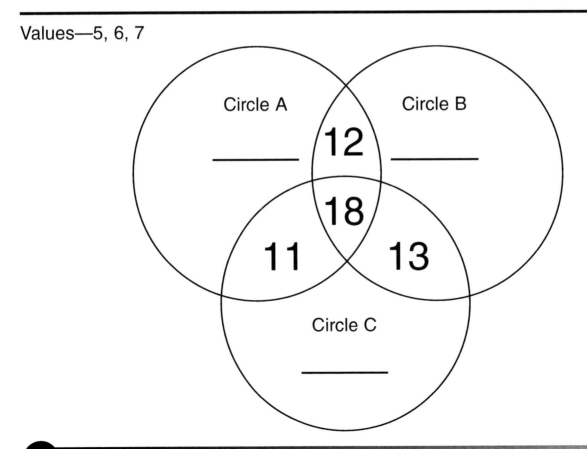

Brain Teaser 24

Mystery Circles Set C

Each circle has a specific value—for example 2, 3, or 4. The sum is where two (or more) circles overlap. Find the value of each circle. Study the example below.

Example: Values—2, 3, 4

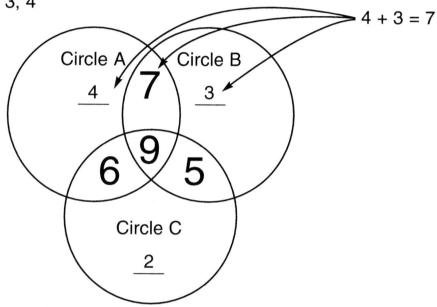

Values—8, 9, 10

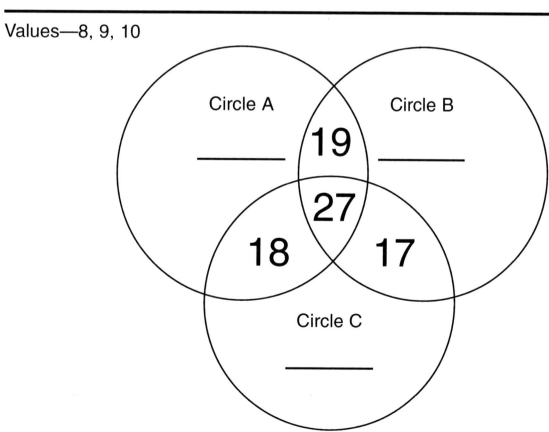

Brain Teaser 25

Mystery Circles Set D

Each circle has a specific value—for example 2, 3, or 4. The product is where two (or more) circles overlap. Find the value of each circle. Study the example below.

Example: Values—2, 3, 4

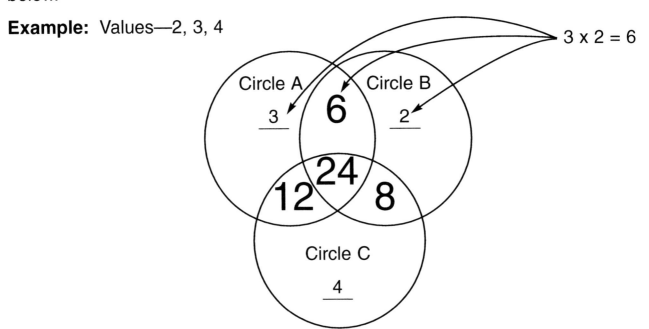

3 x 2 = 6

Values—4, 5, 6

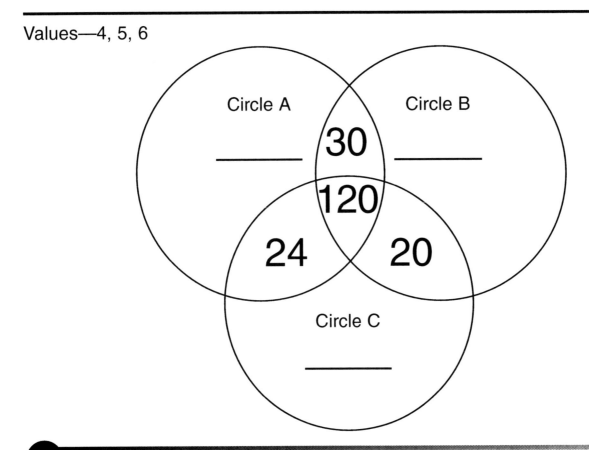

Multiplying Single Digits

Brain Teaser 26

Mystery Circles Set E

Each circle has a specific value—for example 2, 3, or 4. The product is where two (or more) circles overlap. Find the factor of each circle. Study the example below.

Example: Values—2, 3, 4

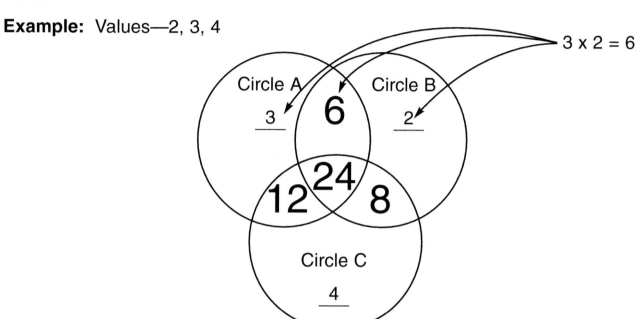

Values—6, 7, 8

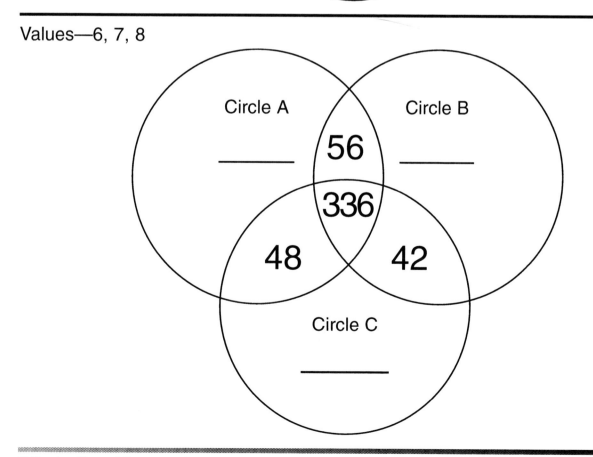

Brain Teaser 27

Mystery Circles Set F

Each circle has a specific value—for example 2, 4, or 16. The quotient is where two (or more) circles overlap. Find the value of each circle. Study the example below.

Example: Values—2, 4, 16

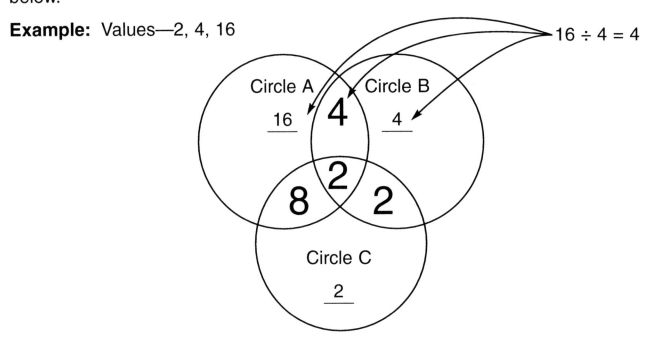

Values—3, 6, 18

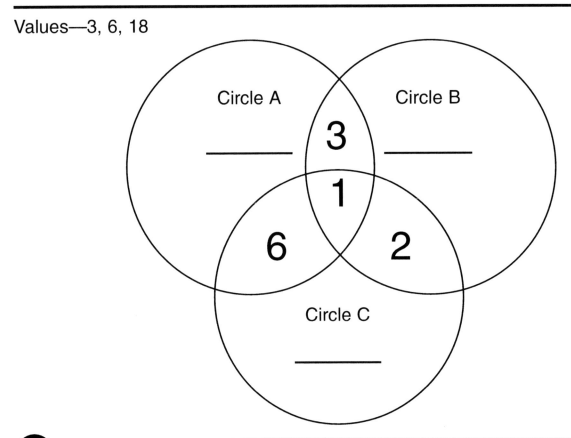

Brain Teaser 28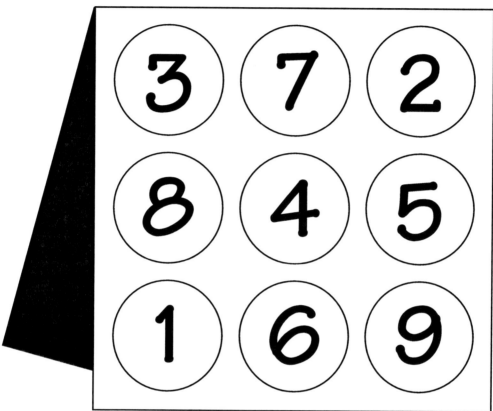

Bean Bag Toss #1

Solve each word problem. The bean bag can hit the same number more than once.

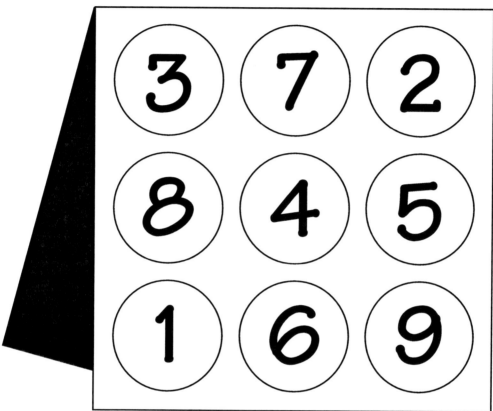

1. Beth had three throws that landed on three different numbers. When the numbers are added together, the answer is 24. What three numbers did she hit? _____, _____, _____	**2.** Cat had two throws. When the two numbers are added together, the answer is 3. What two numbers did she hit? _____ and _____
3. Ryan had three throws and scored the smallest number of points possible. What three numbers did Ryan hit? _____, _____, _____	**4.** Jack had two throws and scored the largest number of points possible. What two numbers did Jack hit? _____ and _____

Brain Teaser 29

Bean Bag Toss #2

Solve each word problem. The bean bag can hit the same number more than once.

1. Thomas threw two bean bags. The difference between the numbers is 3. The smaller number is larger than 16. What two numbers did Thomas hit?

_____ and _____

2. Jan threw two bean bags. The difference between the numbers is 5. The larger number is 17. What is the smaller number?

_____

3. Bill threw two bean bags. The difference between the numbers is 1. Both numbers are less than 14. What are the two numbers?

_____ and _____

4. Wilma threw two bean bags. The difference between the numbers is 4. One of the numbers is 17. What is the other number?

_____

Brain Teaser 30 ꙮꙮꙮꙮꙮꙮꙮꙮꙮꙮꙮꙮ

Bean Bag Toss #3

Solve each word problem. The bean bag can hit the same number more than once.

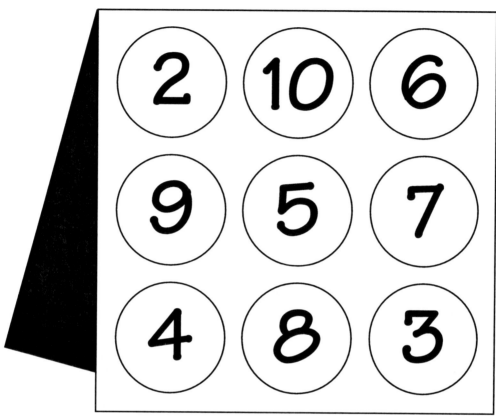

1. Marcus tossed three bean bags. When the numbers are added together the answer is 10. When the numbers are multiplied the product is 30. What are the three numbers? _____, _____, _____

2. Nancy tossed two bean bags. When the numbers are added together the sum is 12. When the smaller number is subtracted from the larger number the difference is 8. When the larger number is divided by the smaller number the quotient is 5. What are the two numbers? _____ and _____

3. Randy tossed two bean bags. When the numbers are added together the sum is 13. When the numbers are multiplied, the product is 42. When the smaller number is subtracted from the larger number, the difference is 1. What are the two numbers? _____ and _____

Brain Teaser 31 🐚 🐚 🐚 🐚 🐚 🐚 🐚 🐚 🐚 🐚 🐚

Bean Bag Toss #4

Solve each word problem. The bean bag can hit the same number more than once.

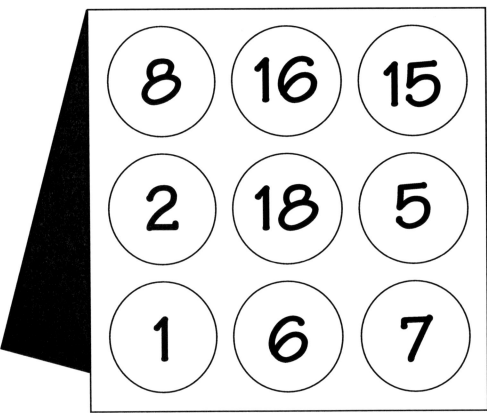

1. Jarod threw two bean bags. One number is two times larger than the other number. Both of the numbers are even numbers. What two numbers did Jarod hit? _____ and _____	2. Brita threw two bean bags. One number is three times larger than the other number. Both of the numbers are odd numbers. What two numbers did Brita hit? _____ and _____
3. Misty threw 2 bean bags. Both numbers are divisible by 6. What two numbers did Misty hit? _____ and _____	4. Dave threw two bean bags and hit an odd and an even number. Both numbers are divisible by 3. When both numbers are added together, the sum is 33. What numbers did Dave hit? _____ and _____

Brain Teaser 32 ෨ ❡ ෨ ❡ ෨ ❡ ෨ ❡ ෨ ෨ ❡

Square-O-Rama 30

Use the numbers in the Number Bank to complete the Square-O-Rama. The numbers in each row and in each column must add together to equal 30. You can only use each number once. (*Hint:* Rewrite the numbers on sticky notes—it makes it easier to rearrange the numbers!)

Number Bank								
6	7	8	9	10	11	12	13	14

Brain Teaser 33

Square-O-Rama 48

Use the numbers in the Number Bank to complete the Square-O-Rama. The numbers in each row and in each column must add together to equal 48. You can only use each number once. (*Hint:* Rewrite the numbers on sticky notes—it makes it easier to rearrange the numbers!)

Number Bank								
12	13	14	15	16	17	18	19	20

Brain Teaser 34 ꙮ ꙮ ꙮ ꙮ ꙮ ꙮ ꙮ ꙮ ꙮ ꙮ ꙮ

Square-O-Rama 96

Use the numbers in the Number Bank to complete the Square-O-Rama. The numbers in each row and in each column must add together to equal 96. You can only use each number once. (*Hint:* Rewrite the numbers on sticky notes—it makes it easier to rearrange the numbers!)

Number Bank								
28	29	30	31	32	33	34	35	36

Brain Teaser 35

Square-O-Rama 120

Use the numbers in the Number Bank to complete the Square-O-Rama. The numbers in each row and in each column must add together to equal 120. You can only use each number once. (*Hint:* Rewrite the numbers on sticky notes—it makes it easier to rearrange the numbers!)

Number Bank								
36	37	38	39	40	41	42	43	44

Brain Teaser 36

Dangerous Dominoes #1

Dominoes were used to create the puzzle. The dominoes are placed vertically and horizontally in the puzzle. Circle each pair of numbers to match the domino used. Each domino was used one time.

Dominoes Used

0 1	1 0	1 3	3 3
3 4	3 5	4 2	4 3

Teaser Brain 37

Dangerous Dominoes #2

Dominoes were used to create the puzzle. The dominoes are placed vertically and horizontally in the puzzle. Circle each pair of numbers to match the domino used. Each domino was used one time.

Dominoes Used

1 1	1 2	4 4	4 5
5 1	5 2	5 3	5 5

Brain Teaser 38

Dangerous Dominoes #3

Dominoes were used to create the puzzle. The dominoes are placed vertically and horizontally in the puzzle. Circle each pair of numbers to match the domino used. Each domino was used one time.

Dominoes Used

0 2	0 4	4 0	5 6
0 3	3 0	5 4	6 1

Brain Teaser 39

Dangerous Dominoes #4

Dominoes were used to create the puzzle. The dominoes are placed vertically and horizontally in the puzzle. Circle each pair of numbers to match the domino used. Each domino was used one time.

Dominoes Used

0 0	0 5	0 6	2 0
2 3	4 1	5 0	6 0

Brain Teaser 40 ා ම ා ම ා ම ා ම ා ා ම

Math Challenge #1

Roll a 6-sided die. Use the number on the die to make a math problem with a total shown on one of the squares. Write the math problem on the square.

Sample problems:

- If the die rolls on "3," a sample equation might be "3" x 6 = 18
- If the die rolls on "5," a sample equation might be "5" x 2 + 4 = 14
- If the die rolls on "1," a sample equation might be 9 ÷ "1" = 9

(*Helpful Hint:* The math problem can also be written on a small sticky note and placed on the square. This will allow the game board to be used many times.)

(*Variation:* Play against a classmate. The first player to get four squares in a row—vertically, horizontally, or diagonally—wins the game!)

1	2	3	4	5
16	17	18	19	6
15	24	25	20	7
14	23	22	21	8
13	12	11	10	9

Brain Teaser 41 ᔕ ᑕᔕ ᔕ ᑕᔕ ᔕ ᑕᔕ ᔕ ᑕᔕ ᔕ ᔕ ᑕᔕ

Math Challenge #2

Roll a 6-sided die. Use the number on the die to make a math problem with a total shown on one of the squares. Write the math problem on the square.

Sample problems:

- If the die rolls on "3," a sample equation might be "3" x 6 = 18
- If the die rolls on "5," a sample equation might be "5" x 2 + 4 = 14
- If the die rolls on "1," a sample equation might be 9 ÷ "1" = 9

(*Helpful Hint:* The math problem can also be written on a small sticky note and placed on the square. This will allow the game board to be used many times.)

(*Variation:* Play against a classmate. The first player to get four squares in a row—vertically, horizontally, or diagonally—wins the game!)

73	42	16	84	79
89	51	41	2	72
31	12	14	95	67
62	85	35	93	25
88	65	37	58	90

Brain Teaser 42

What Comes Next?

Write the missing number.

A. 1, 2, 4, 8, 16, _____, _____

B. 100, 50, 90, 45, 80, 40, _____, _____

C. 1, 2, 4, 7, 11, 16, 22, 29, _____, _____

D. 100, 99, 97, 94, 90, _____, _____

E. 3, 9, 27, _____, _____

F. 51, 62, 74, 87, _____, _____

G. 11, 22, 33, 44, 55, 66, _____, _____

Brain Teaser 43

Solve It!

You have been asked to audition for a television quiz show called *Number Trivia.* The television producer asks you to solve the following problem:

- Circle sets of three numbers that add up to eight.

- You can only circle each number once.

- When circling numbers you may not cross another line.

- You must use all of the numbers.

2	0	8	0	1
1	5	4	7	0
3	1	3	5	1
4	1	1	5	2
7	0	0	2	0
1	8	0	7	1

Answer Key

Page 4
Color red: 27, 35, 49, 93, 31, 65, 5, 13, 47
Color blue: 18, 24, 16, 90, 38, 88, 76, 2, 22, 54

Page 5
Color orange: 77, 91, 98, 76, 52, 88, 61, 54, 73, 87, 71, 91, 75, 53, 62
Color green: 31, 49, 6, 10, 9, 21, 11, 1, 8, 10, 35, 32
Larger numbers: 81, 86, 63, 99, 94, 82, 89
Smaller numbers: 10, 14, 19, 33, 29, 44

Page 6
Color red: 2, 3, 6, 12, 4, 1, 6
Color green: 5, 14, 13, 25, 8, 10, 11, 9, 85, 7
Factors of 16: 4, 8, 2
Factors of 20: 10, 2, 5, 4

Page 7
Color blue: all 1s, 2s, 3s, and 9s
1. 1, 2, 4
2. 1, 2, 3, 6
3. 1, 3, 9
4. 1, 2, 5, 10
5. 1, 3, 5, 15
Color black: 4, 5, 7, 10, 11, 13

Page 8
1. $7 \times 3 = 21$
2. $12 + 10 = 22$
3. $12 - 6 = 6$
4. $10 \div 5 = 2$
5. Answers will vary. Sample answer: $2002 \times 4 = 8008$
6. Answers will vary. Sample answer: $1966 - 30 = 1936$

7. $3 + 7 = 10$
8. Answers will vary. Sample answer: (559) 123-4567 would be $5 + 5 + 9 + 1 + 2 + 3 + 4 + 5 + 6 + 7 = 47$
9. Answers will vary. Sample answer: $2002 - 1966 = 36$
10. Answers will vary. Sample answer: 36 (age) x 30 (date of birth) = 1,080

Page 9
1. $4 \times 1 = 4$
2. $2 \times 4 = 8$
3. $8 \div 2 = 4$
4. $6 \times 8 = 48$
5. $3 \times 2 = 6$
6. $2 \div 1 = 2$
7. $8 - 4 = 4$
8. $2 \times 0 = 0$
9. $0 + 0 = 0$
10. $2 + 1 = 3$

Page 10
1. $5 + 6 = 11$
2. $10 - 4 = 6$
3. $25 \div 1 = 25$
4. $1 \times 5 = 5$
5. $3 \times 4 = 12$
6. $6 - 3 = 3$
7. $10 - 10 = 0$
8. $1 + 5 = 6$
9. $9 \div 3 = 3$
10. $1 \times 100 = 100$

Page 11
1. $12 \times 7 = 84$
2. $12 \div 2 = 6$
3. $1 \times 3 = 3$
4. $2 \times 12 = 24$
5. $12 \div 6 = 2$
6. $3 \times 10 = 30$
7. $10 \times 10 = 100$
8. $3 - 1 = 2$

9. $365 + 120 = 485$
10. $7 - 2 = 5$

Page 12
Check to make sure the student has colored factors that equal 12.

Page 13
Check to make sure the student has colored factors that equal 18.

Page 14
Check to make sure the student has colored factors that equal 24.

Page 15
Check to make sure the student has colored factors that equal 30.

Page 16
Orange jelly beans: 10
Green jelly beans: 15
Black jelly beans: 25
Yellow jelly beans: 40
Pink jelly beans: 25
White jelly beans: 30
1. black and pink
2. 165 jelly beans
3. more red and yellow jelly beans

Page 17
Puzzle #1

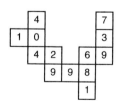

Puzzle #2

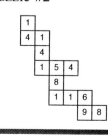

Page 18
Puzzle #3

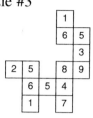

Puzzle #4

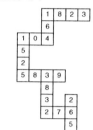

Page 19
Puzzle #5

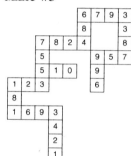

Page 20
Puzzle #6

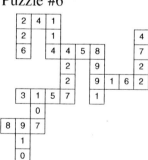

Page 21
Puzzle #7

Answer Key (cont.)

Page 22
Clyde has $50.00;
Cybil has $10.00;
Val has $5.00;
Ty has $1.00;
Angel has $20.00

Page 23
Charles spent $1.49;
Lorne spent $1.39;
Celia spent $1.19;
Bo spent $1.29;
Libby spent $1.59

Page 24
Henry's lucky number
is 37; Selina's lucky
number is 88; Travis'
lucky number is 47;
Emilio's lucky number
is 29; Mavis' lucky
number is 18; Sarah's
lucky number is 41.

Page 25

Circle A: 2
Circle B: 3
Circle C: 1

Page 26
Circle A: 5
Circle B: 7
Circle C: 6

Page 27
Circle A: 10
Circle B: 9
Circle C: 8

Page 28
Circle A: 6
Circle B: 5
Circle C: 4

Page 29
Circle A: 8
Circle B: 7
Circle C: 6

Page 30
Circle A: 18
Circle B: 6
Circle C: 3

Page 31
1. 7, 8, 9
2. 1, 2
3. 1, 1, 1
4. 9, 9

Page 32
1. 17, 20
2. 12
3. 13, 12
4. 13

Page 33
1. 2, 5, 3
2. 10, 2
3. 6, 7

Page 34
1. 8, 16
2. 5, 15
3. 6, 18
4. 15, 18

Page 35
Sample solution
   Top row: 10, 12, 8
   Middle row: 6, 11, 13
   Bottom row: 14, 7, 9

Page 36
Sample solution
   Top row: 16, 18, 14
   Middle row: 12, 17, 19
   Bottom row: 20, 13, 15

Page 37
Sample solution
   Top row: 32, 34, 30
   Middle row: 28, 33, 35
   Bottom row: 36, 29, 31

Page 38
Sample solution
   Top row: 40, 42, 38
   Middle row: 36, 41, 43
   Bottom row: 44, 37, 39

Page 39
Sample solution

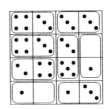

Page 40
Sample solution

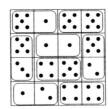

Page 41
Sample solution

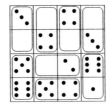

Page 42
Sample solution

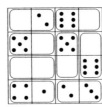

Page 43
Answers will vary.

Page 44
Answers will vary.

Page 45
A. 32, 64
B. 70, 35
C. 37, 46
D. 85, 79
E. 81, 243
F. 101, 116
G. 77, 88

Page 46

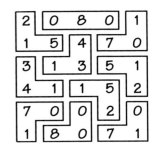